# SEX IS A GA

## BY BOB ZAHN

## CCC PUBLICATIONS

Published by:
CCC Publications
1111 Rancho Conejo Blvd.
Suites 411 & 412
Newbury Park, CA 91320

Manufactured in the United States of America

Cover © 1996 CCC Publications

Interior illustrations © 1996 CCC Publications

Cover & interior art by Bob Zahn

Cover/Interior production by Oasis Graphics

ISBN: 1-57644-003-6

If your local U.S. bookstore is out of stock, copies of this book may be obtained by mailing check or money order for $5.95 per book (plus $2.75 to cover postage and handling) to: CCC Publications; 1111 Rancho Conejo Blvd.; Suites 411 & 412; Newbury Park, CA 91320.

Pre-publication Edition - 7/96

First Printing - 7/99

# INTRODUCTION

**SEX** IS THE WORLD'S MOST POPULAR **INDOOR** GAME.
IN FACT, IT'S BECOMING THE MOST POPULAR **OUTDOOR** GAME.
AND, WITHOUT A DOUBT, IT'S THE MOST POPULAR
**CONTACT** GAME!

Dedicated to Donna

"IF SEX IS A GAME I'M SCORELESS!"

"...BUT FIRST, OUR NATIONAL ANTHEM."

"PLAY ME OR TRADE ME!"

"I'VE BEEN VOTED 'MOST VALUABLE PLAYER'
IN OUR WIFE SWAPPING CLUB!"

"HOW COME YOU ALWAYS LAND THE **BIG** ONES?"

"MY WIFE AND MY BEST BUDDY! WHAT IN HELL ARE YOU DOING HERE, BURT? YOU MISSED THE BIG GAME!"

"NO, I DON'T WANT YOU TO SLAM-DUNK IT!"

"MY WIFE SENT ME HERE TO BUY AN EXERCISE VIDEO.
DO YOU HAVE ANY X-RATED ONES?"

"THAT'S THE FIRST TIME I EVER PLAYED FULL-CONTACT STRIP POKER!"

"RATS! I EJACULATED WHILE I WAS WARMING UP TO COME IN."

"ARE YOU GOING TO PRACTICE YOUR PUTTING ALL NIGHT?"

"CAN YOUR WIFE COME OUT TO PLAY?"

"THAT'S MY HUSBAND. HE LIKES TO WATCH."

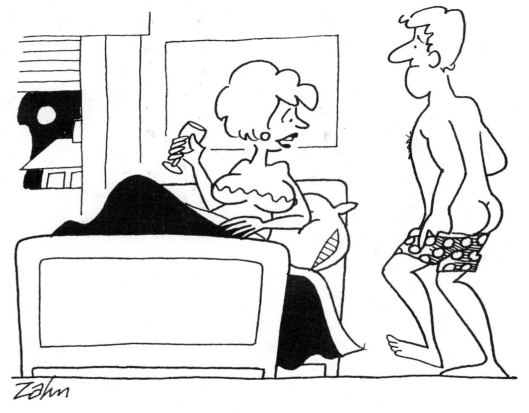

"YOU MEAN WHEN YOU SAID 'LONG AND STRAIGHT'
YOU WERE TALKING ABOUT YOUR GOLF GAME!"

"THAT'S MY GIRLFRIEND."

"WHAT'S THIS RUMOR I HEAR ABOUT ONE OF THE CHEERLEADERS GOING **UP** ON YOU?"

"BUT YOU PLAY DOUBLE-HEADERS ALL THE TIME IN BASEBALL!"

"THEY OBVIOUSLY DON'T KNOW SQUAT ABOUT SURFING!"

"THERE'S NO SPORTS ON TV . . . YOU WANT TO MAKE LOVE?"

"THIS SOUNDS LIKE A GOOD ONE. IT BURNS 400 CALORIES AN HOUR!"

"YOU TOLD ME YOU WERE TAKING ME TO A COCK FIGHT . . .
THAT'S JUST A COUPLE OF CHICKENS FIGHTING!"

"WANT TO SEE MY SNATCH?"

"HOW COME WE ALWAYS HAVE TO BE **SKINS?**"

"I KNEW YOU WERE A RUNNER, BUT I DIDN'T KNOW YOU WERE **THAT** FAST!"

"I'LL HELP YOU WITH YOUR HOMEWORK IF YOU HELP ME WITH MY SEX LIFE."

"IF THAT WAS A BALL GAME I WOULD HAVE SENT YOU TO THE SHOWERS!"

"YOU BOTH KNOW THE RULES – NO KICKING, NO BITING, NO GOUGING AND NO MUSHY STUFF."

"THAT'S A RECORD . . . FOR THE FEWEST STROKES EVER TAKEN ON ME!"

"Hi!"

"WOW! A MINUTE AND A HALF . . . I JUST TOPPED
MY PERSONAL BEST BY TWO SECONDS!"

"IF WE TRADED OUR WHITE GODDESS TO ANOTHER TRIBE ABOUT THE BEST WE'D GET FOR HER WOULD BE A SIXTH ROUND DRAFT CHOICE."

"THIS IS THE WXXX ELEVEN O'CLOCK TOPLESS SPORTS NEWS . . ."

"I'M TRYING TO GET MYSELF INTO SHAPE AND SHE'S THE SHAPE I'M TRYING TO GET MYSELF INTO!"

"YOU LIKE AN OVERSIZED RACQUET WHEN YOU PLAY TENNIS AND I LIKE ONE WHEN WE HAVE SEX!"

"WE HAD 'SHOW AND TELL' IN SEX EDUCATION TODAY
AND I PULLED A BONER!"

"TIME OUT! I'VE GOT A CRAMP!"

"THAT'S THE ONLY EXERCISE VIDEO I'VE EVER SEEN WHERE THE WOMEN DON'T WEAR BRAS!"

"HOW WOULD YOU LIKE TO PUT YOUR GRIP ON THOSE BEAUTIES?"

"I WOULD THINK AN OLD FISHERMAN LIKE YOU WOULD BE ABLE TO RECOGNIZE ARTIFICIAL LURES!"

"NICE TITS!"

CHARLIE WAS HEADED FOR THE BATHROOM FOR HIS DAILY EXERCISE.

"FIRST THING YOU HAVE TO DO IS KEEP YOUR EYE ON THE BALL ..."

"HOW ABOUT A LITTLE **SEX**ERCISE?"

"DAMN IT! WILL YOU BACK OFF A LITTLE!"

"WOW! WHAT A GREAT GAME! THAT'S THE THIRD TIME THAT CHEERLEADER'S BOOB HAS COME OUT!"

"IF YOU'RE NOT IN THE BEDROOM IN TWO MINUTES
I'M STARTING THE GAME WITHOUT YOU!"

"I TAKE IT THIS IS GOING TO BE A QUICKIE?"

"I'M A SLICER, SHE'S A HOOKER!"

"I PLAY A LOT OF SPORTS."

"LET'S RUN THROUGH THIS CHECKLIST. I TOOK THE PILL, YOU GOT THE RUBBER AND THE FOAM, I PUT THE DIAPHRAGM IN, GOT THE LUBE CREAM AND THE TISSUES . . ."

"I'M GAME."

"I LIKE TO KEEP ACCURATE RECORDS IN MY DIARY."

"YOU REMEMBER . . . AFTER THE SUPER BOWL LAST YEAR?"

"SHE HAD A NO-HITTER GOING UNTIL I SNUCK UP ON HER!"

"DAMN! I WAS GOING TO PLAY GOLF TODAY. MY WHOLE DAY IS RUINED!"

"I GOT A COUPLE OF VIDEOS THAT ALWAYS MAKE YOU HOT! SUPER BOWL AND WORLD SERIES HIGHLIGHTS."

"IN YOUR WILDEST DREAMS!"

"I ONLY JOG TO BE SOCIAL."

WALTER SCORES!

"I SUGGEST YOU STOP SUCKING ON WOMEN'S TOES . . .
AT LEAST UNTIL I CAN CLEAR UP THAT ATHLETE'S TONGUE."

"I DON'T CARE IF YOU DO CHEW WHEN YOU'RE PLAYING BALL!
YOU'RE NOT CHEWING WHEN YOU'RE BALLING ME!"

"AND HOW LONG HAVE YOU HAD A BLACK BELT IN KARATE,
MS. MEYERS?"

"WILL YOU STOP THAT HOLLERING SO I CAN HEAR THIS SCORE?"

"SO WHY ARE YOU WAITING UNTIL HALFTIME?
YOU ONLY LAST THROUGH **ONE** COMMERCIAL."

"WE DON'T HAVE ANY OPENINGS FOR CHEERLEADERS –
BUT ARE YOU INTERESTED IN BEING 'TEAM MASCOT'?"

"DO YOU FANTASIZE ABOUT OTHER WOMEN WHEN WE MAKE LOVE?"

"I'M RECYCLING SOME CONDOMS."

"IT'S A GOOD THING THERE'S NOT A SIZE LIMIT ON THOSE THINGS OR I'D HAVE TO THROW YOU BACK."

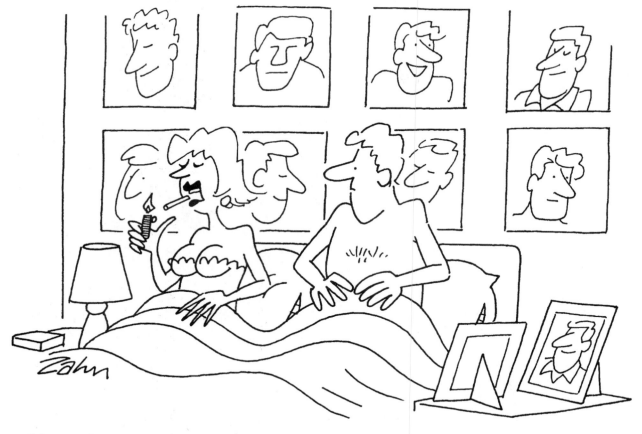

"I'M SORRY, RALPH, BUT YOU DIDN'T MAKE THE FINAL CUT."

# TITLES BY CCC PUBLICATIONS

**Blank Books ($3.99)**
SEX AFTER BABY
SEX AFTER 30
SEX AFTER 40
SEX AFTER 50

**Retail $4.95 – $4.99**
"?" book
CAN SEX IMPROVE YOUR GOLF?
THE COMPLETE BOOGER BOOK
FLYING FUNNIES
MARITAL BLISS & OXYMORONS
THE ADULT DOT-TO-DOT BOOK
THE DEFINITIVE FART BOOK
THE COMPLETE WIMP'S GUIDE TO SEX
THE CAT OWNER'S SHAPE UP MANUAL
THE OFFICE FROM HELL
FITNESS FANATICS
YOUNGER MEN ARE BETTER THAN RETIN-A
BUT OSSIFER, IT'S NOT MY FAULT
YOU KNOW YOU'RE AN OLD FART WHEN...
1001 WAYS TO PROCRASTINATE
HORMONES FROM HELL II
SHARING THE ROAD WITH IDIOTS
THE GREATEST ANSWERING MACHINE MESSAGES
WHAT DO WE DO NOW??
HOW TO TALK YOU WAY OUT OF A TRAFFIC TICKET
THE BOTTOM HALF
LIFE'S MOST EMBARRASSING MOMENTS
HOW TO ENTERTAIN PEOPLE YOU HATE
YOUR GUIDE TO CORPORATE SURVIVAL
NO HANG-UPS (Volumes I, II & III – $3.95 ea.)
TOTALLY OUTRAGEOUS BUMPER-SNICKERS ($2.95)

**Retail $5.95**
30 – DEAL WITH IT!
40 – DEAL WITH IT!
50 – DEAL WITH IT!
60 – DEAL WITH IT!
OVER THE HILL – DEAL WITH IT!
SLICK EXCUSES FOR STUPID SCREW-UPS
SINGLE WOMEN VS. MARRIED WOMEN
TAKE A WOMAN'S WORD FOR IT
SEXY CROSSWORD PUZZLES
SO, YOU'RE GETTING MARRIED
YOU KNOW HE'S A WOMANIZING SLIMEBALL WHEN...
GETTING OLD SUCKS
WHY GOD MAKES BALD GUYS
OH BABY!
PMS CRAZED: TOUCH ME AND I'LL KILL YOU!
WHY MEN ARE CLUELESS
THE BOOK OF WHITE TRASH
THE ART OF MOONING
GOLFAHOLICS
CRINKLED 'N' WRINKLED
SMART COMEBACKS FOR STUPID QUESTIONS
YIKES! IT'S ANOTHER BIRTHDAY
SEX IS A GAME
SEX AND YOUR STARS
SIGNS YOUR SEX LIFE IS DEAD
MALE BASHING: WOMEN'S FAVORITE PASTIME
THINGS YOU CAN DO WITH A USELESS MAN
MORE THINGS YOU CAN DO WITH A USELESS MAN
RETIREMENT: THE GET EVEN YEARS
LITTLE INSTRUCTION BOOK OF THE RICH & FAMOUS
WELCOME TO YOUR MIDLIFE CRISIS
GETTING EVEN WITH THE ANSWERING MACHINE
ARE YOU A SPORTS NUT?
MEN ARE PIGS / WOMEN ARE BITCHES
THE BETTER HALF
ARE WE DYSFUNCTIONAL YET?
TECHNOLOGY BYTES!
50 WAYS TO HUSTLE YOUR FRIENDS

HORMONES FROM HELL
HUSBANDS FROM HELL
KILLER BRAS & Other Hazards Of The 50's
IT'S BETTER TO BE OVER THE HILL THAN UNDER IT
HOW TO REALLY PARTY!!!
WORK SUCKS!
THE PEOPLE WATCHER'S FIELD GUIDE
THE ABSOLUTE LAST CHANCE DIET BOOK
THE UGLY TRUTH ABOUT MEN
NEVER A DULL CARD
THE LITTLE BOOK OF ROMANTIC LIES

**Retail $6.95**
CYBERGEEK IS CHIC
THE DIFFERENCE BETWEEN MEN AND WOMEN
GO TO HEALTH!
NOT TONIGHT, DEAR, I HAVE A COMPUTER!
THINGS YOU WILL NEVER HEAR THEM SAY
THE SENIOR CITIZENS'S SURVIVAL GUIDE
IT'S A MAD MAD MAD SPORTS WORLD
THE LITTLE BOOK OF CORPORATE LIES
RED HOT MONOGAMY
LOVE DAT CAT
HOW TO SURVIVE A JEWISH MOTHER

**Retail $7.95**
WHY MEN DON'T HAVE A CLUE
LADIES, START YOUR ENGINES!
ULI STEIN'S "ANIMAL LIFE"
ULI STEIN'S "I'VE GOT IT BUT IT'S JAMMED"
ULI STEIN'S "THAT SHOULD NEVER HAVE HAPPENED"

**NO HANG-UPS – CASSETTES Retail $5.98**
Vol. I:     GENERAL MESSAGES (M or F)
Vol. II:    BUSINESS MESSAGES (M or F)
Vol. III:   'R' RATED MESSAGES (M or F)
Vol. V:     CELEBRI-TEASE